The **Tower**
of **Babel**

The origin and dispersal of the nations

Acknowledgments

Dr. Elizabeth Mitchell, Frost Smith, Dr. Russell Fuller,
Dr. Andrew Snelling, Ken Ham, Troy Lacey, David Wright,
Steve Fazekas, and Steve Golden.

Second Edition

Reprinted June 2022

Print ISBN: 978-1-9844-0927-0
ebook ISBN: 978-1-9844-1072-6

Cover Design: Jenn Reed
Interior Design: Michaela Duncan
Editing: Ryan Freeman & Evonne Krell

Printed in China

AnswersInGenesis.org

Table **of Contents**

Introduction

Genesis 1–11 is under attack in today's culture. In many cases, we read of attacks on Genesis 1 and 2 where attempts are made to add millions of years to the creation week.[1] We see attacks on the fall of mankind in Genesis 3 where there is a denial of the reality of Adam and Eve, original sin, and the need for a Savior. We observe further attacks with the denial of Satan's involvement by claiming he is not real.[2]

We see attacks on Genesis 4 and 5 with alleged gaps in the genealogies and attempts to squeeze thousands of years into them (even though this does not help the case for millions of years).[3] Genesis 6–9 have come under attack, with some claiming the flood was just a local event and reinterpreting flood rock layers as evidence for millions of years.[4]

Genesis 10 and 11 are under severe attack as well. Scholars write off what occurred at the tower of Babel as mythology and deny that it was a historical event. Join me as we dive into the Bible and look into history and theology in a God-honoring fashion to refute these attacks.

---

1 A book that tackles this subject is Ken Ham's *The Lie: Evolution/Millions of Years* (Green Forest, AR: Master Books, 2012).

2 A book that addresses attacks on Genesis 3 is Bodie Hodge's *The Fall of Satan* (Green Forest, AR: Master Books, 2011).

3 There are three chapters that deal with this in *The New Answers Book 2*, Ken Ham, gen. ed. (Green Forest, AR: Master Books, 2008): "How old is the earth?" by Bodie Hodge, "Are there gaps in the Genesis genealogies?" by Larry Pierce and Ken Ham, and "Doesn't Egyptian chronology prove that the Bible is unreliable?" by Dr. Elizabeth Mitchell.

4 There are numerous books that tackle this subject from the time-honored classic *The Genesis Flood* by Drs. Henry Morris and John Whitcomb to Dr. Andrew Snelling's treatise *Earth's Catastrophic Past*. Also, *The New Answers Books 1, 2*, and *3* have a number of chapters discussing these attacks.

THE FIRST BOOK OF MOSES

COMMONLY CALLED

GENESIS

In the beginning God created
the heavens and the earth. 2 The
th was without form and void, and
ness was upon the face of t
dee and the Spirit of God was m
ing the face of the waters.
3 God said, "Let there
e was light. 4And
was good; and
rated the light Dav
called the Night
vening and there
God said

The Biblical Account

Genesis 11:1–9

[1] Now the whole earth had one language and the same words. [2] And as people migrated from the east, they found a plain in the land of Shinar and settled there. [3] And they said to one another, "Come, let us make bricks, and burn them thoroughly." And they had brick for stone, and bitumen for mortar. [4] Then they said, "Come, let us build ourselves a city and a tower with its top in the heavens, and let us make a name for ourselves, lest we be dispersed over the face of the whole earth." [5] And the LORD came down to see the city and the tower, which the children of man had built. [6] And the LORD said, "Behold, they are one people, and they have all one language, and this is only the beginning of what they will do. And nothing that they propose to do will now be impossible for them. [7] Come, let us go down and there confuse their language, so that they may not understand one another's speech." [8] So the LORD dispersed them from there over the face of all the earth, and they left off building the city. [9] Therefore its name was called Babel, because there the LORD confused the language of all the earth. And from there the LORD dispersed them over the face of all the earth.

Next, we insert the genealogies of Noah's three sons. Their descendants gathered together at Babel and built a tower. They were involved when the confusion occurred. This is the division of their familial genealogies, allotted lands, and language splitting.

Genesis 10

[1] These are the generations of the sons of Noah, Shem, Ham, and Japheth. Sons were born to them after the flood.

Descendants of Japheth

[2] The sons of Japheth: Gomer, Magog, Madai, Javan, Tubal, Meshech, and Tiras. [3] The sons of Gomer: Ashkenaz, Riphath, and Togarmah. [4] The sons of Javan: Elishah, Tarshish, Kittim, and Dodanim. [5] From these the coastland peoples spread in their lands, each with his own language, by their clans, in their nations.

Descendants of Ham

[6] The sons of Ham: Cush, Egypt, Put, and Canaan. [7] The sons of Cush: Seba, Havilah, Sabtah, Raamah, and Sabteca. The sons of Raamah: Sheba and Dedan. [8] Cush fathered Nimrod; he was the first on earth to be a mighty man. [9] He was a mighty hunter before the Lord. Therefore it is said, "Like Nimrod a mighty hunter before the Lord." [10] The beginning of his kingdom was Babel, Erech, Accad, and Calneh, in the land of Shinar. [11] From that land he went into Assyria and built Nineveh, Rehoboth-Ir, Calah, and [12] Resen between Nineveh and Calah; that is the great city. [13] Egypt fathered Ludim, Anamim, Lehabim, Naphtuhim, [14] Pathrusim, Casluhim (from whom the Philistines came), and Caphtorim. [15] Canaan fathered Sidon his firstborn and Heth, [16] and the Jebusites, the Amorites, the Girgashites, [17] the Hivites, the Arkites, the Sinites, [18] the Arvadites, the Zemarites, and the Hamathites. Afterward the clans of the Canaanites dispersed. [19] And the territory of the Canaanites extended from Sidon in the direction of Gerar as far as Gaza, and in the direction of Sodom, Gomorrah, Admah, and Zeboiim, as far as Lasha. [20] These are the sons of Ham, by their clans, their languages, their lands, and their nations.

Descendants of Shem

²¹ To Shem also, the father of all the children of Eber, the elder brother of Japheth, the children were born. ²² The sons of Shem: Elam, Asshur, Arpachshad, Lud, and Aram. ²³ The sons of Aram: Uz, Hul, Gether, and Mash. ²⁴ Arpachshad fathered Shelah; and Shelah fathered Eber. ²⁵ To Eber were born two sons: the name of the one was Peleg, for in his days the earth was divided, and his brother's name was Joktan. ²⁶ Joktan fathered Almodad, Sheleph, Hazarmaveth, Jerah, ²⁷ Hadoram, Uzal, Diklah, ²⁸ Obal, Abimael, Sheba, ²⁹ Ophir, Havilah, and Jobab; all these were the sons of Joktan. ³⁰ The territory in which they lived extended from Mesha in the direction of Sephar to the hill country of the east. ³¹ These are the sons of Shem, by their clans, their languages, their lands, and their nations. ³² These are the clans of the sons of Noah, according to their genealogies, in their nations, and from these the nations spread abroad on the earth after the flood.

Is There a Contradiction Between Genesis 10 and 11?

Isn't there a contradiction between Genesis 10 (world having multiple languages) and 11 (world having one language)?

Problems

A number of people have brought up what seems like an insurmountable objection—the supposed contradiction between Genesis 10 and 11. Genesis 10 clearly says that people were separated according to their languages (plural), while Genesis 11 says that there was only one language until after the incident at the tower of Babel. How do we explain this alleged contradiction?

In Genesis 11:1, the account begins, "Now the whole earth had one language and the same words." But in chapter 10, it reads:

> ⁵ From these the coastland peoples spread in their lands, *each with his own language*, by their clans, in their nations.

> ²⁰ These are the sons of Ham, by their clans, *their languages*, their lands, and their nations.

> ³¹ These are the sons of Shem, by their clans, *their languages*, their lands, and their nations.

In fact, one variation of this alleged contradiction is based on Genesis 11:2, where everyone dwelt in the same place, a plain in the land of Shinar. And yet in chapter 10 we find people divided into their various lands.

The Solution

So how is this resolved? Actually, it is quite simple. Genesis 11:1–9 is the chronological account of the events that occurred. Genesis 10 is the significance or the result of what happened. In other words, Genesis 10 *does not precede* the events in Genesis 11; it just *summarizes and introduces* those events. Genesis 10 sums up *what* happened; Genesis 11 tells *how* it happened.

The opening ("these are the generations of") and closing of Genesis 10 ("these are the clans of the sons of Noah") indicate that the material in between is a genealogy or breakdown of the families. This material fills in extra detail, which here includes the actual division of the languages by respective family groups, or clans, as a result of the splitting up of the earth in Genesis 11:1–9.

This type of thing was common in Hebrew. For example, Genesis 1:1–2:3 is the chronological account of creation. Then the rest of Genesis 2 is a breakdown of the events occurring on day six of creation. The second chapter gives more details of something that happened during creation week. In a like manner, Genesis 10 gives more detail of something that happened in Genesis 11:1–9.

So the solution presents itself when reading the passages: one is chronological (Genesis 11:1–9) and the other is a breakdown of what happened as a result of the linguistic division (Genesis 10). It simply confuses some people because of the placement of chapter 10 prior to chapter 11.

This arrangement serves another purpose. After Genesis 11:1–9, we immediately dive into the genealogy of Shem and follow it to Abraham, where the rest of the Old Testament continues to build. If Genesis 10 were placed between Genesis 11:9–10, it would be an awkward switch since the Genesis 11 genealogies pick up with a different style. Unlike the Genesis 10 genealogies, the ones in Genesis 11 include *chronological* data down to Abraham. By placing Genesis 10 before Genesis 11:1–9, Moses was clearly making a distinction by how these were edited together.

Why Were the People Disobedient?

People have asked, "Why was God so mean that he came down and inflicted such confusion on those innocent people at Babel?"

First, God is a fair judge and does not inflict judgment on anyone without cause. Second, none of us are innocent, and all of us have fallen short ever since the entrance of sin in Genesis 3. And by rights, we should be asking the question "Why is the Lord so patient with us, considering that even one sin is worthy of the judgment of a perfectly holy God?"

Many people today fail to read much of the Bible and know precious little about the character of God. So if someone asks you this question, try not to be taken aback. Rather, be patient with them.

To answer this, we need to jump back to Genesis 9 because the people at Babel were being utterly disobedient:

> And God blessed Noah and his sons and said to them, "Be fruitful and multiply and fill the earth." (Genesis 9:1)

This is reiterated later in Genesis 9:

> And you, be fruitful and multiply, increase greatly on the earth and multiply in it. (Genesis 9:7)

The descendants of Noah were to be fruitful, multiply, and fill the earth. In fact, the descendants of Noah knew this command very well:

> Then they said, "Come, let us build ourselves a city and a tower with its top in the heavens, and let us make a name

for ourselves, lest we be dispersed over the face of the whole earth." (Genesis 11:4)

Notice in verse 4 how they said, "lest we be dispersed over the face of the whole earth." They were *intentionally* trying to defy God. They knew God's command and were trying to go against him. This is sin (disobedience to God).

How is it that they knew this command? Surely Noah and his sons passed this information along to them. Noah was a preacher, or herald, of righteousness (2 Peter 2:5).[1] We often think of Noah preaching against the pre-flood world, and that was indeed the case, as Peter discussed. But there is a little known secret about most preachers . . . they preach until they die! In other words, once a preacher, always a preacher!

Another point of disobedience at Babel is found in Genesis 11:4 and is a *heart* problem. They wanted to make a name for themselves. They were not looking out for others, but for themselves. This is reminiscent of what was going on before the flood. Those wicked people before the flood were "men of renown" (Genesis 6:4).[2] They too were trying to make a name for themselves, and the result was ultimately tremendous violence. The good thing at Babel was that it had not turned to that . . . yet. In retrospect, the judgment at Babel was actually a very mild judgment that was a repercussion of disobedience inflicted on the people to merely confuse their languages.[3]

And there is no doubt that a preacher of righteousness, even after the flood, was able to teach the people what self-centeredness regarding making a name for themselves could lead to. This may have been why the descendants of Noah knew the command to be fruitful, multiply, and fill the earth and the warnings about the pre-flood world's intoxication with fame.

When we examine the genealogies after the flood in Genesis 5, we see that Noah lived for 350 years after the flood, which is plenty of time to pass this information along to his descendants. And the events at the tower of Babel occurred far sooner than Noah's death in the days of Peleg (Genesis 10:25). And that brings us to the question of *when* the scattering occurred.

---

1 2 Peter 2:5—"If he did not spare the ancient world, but preserved Noah, a herald of righteousness, with seven others, when he brought a flood upon the world of the ungodly."

2 Genesis 6:4—"The Nephilim were on the earth in those days, and also afterward, when the sons of God came in to the daughters of man and they bore children to them. These were the mighty men who were of old, the men of renown."

3 When we think of judgments, we often think of the severe ones, such as the curse, the flood, the destruction of Sodom and Gomorrah, or the conquest of the Canaanites, but not all judgments are of this severity. Many judgments in the Bible were not too severe (e.g., Exodus 21).

When Did the Scattering Occur?

Renowned chronologist Archbishop James Ussher[1] placed the time of Babel at 106 years after the flood, near the time Peleg was born.[2] Although this may not be the exact date, it is in range because Peleg was in the fourth generation after the flood, as we read in Genesis 10:

> To Eber were born two sons: the name of the one was Peleg, for in his days the earth was divided, and his brother's name was Joktan. (Genesis 10:25)

Before examining this date in more detail, a common misconception must be dispelled about Genesis 10:25. An extended analysis of this appears in Tower of Babel, but due to the context, it needs to be addressed in short form here.

Continental Split?

Some have suggested that Genesis 10:25 refers to a geophysical splitting of the continents; however, any major continental movements would have been associated with the flood of Noah's time—not the events at Babel. The massive amounts of water and the crustal breakup indicated in Genesis 7:11[3] ("the fountains of the great deep burst forth") were substantial enough to cause catastrophic movements of plates.

Continental collision formations, resulting in high mountains, already existed prior to Peleg's day. For example, we know the mountains of Ararat had formed by the end of the flood because the ark landed there. These mountains were produced by a collision with the Arabian plate and the Eurasian plate. Therefore, the crustal movement must have already occurred by the time the flood ended.

Continental splitting during the day of Peleg would have been catastrophic enough to cause another global flood! Instead, the division mentioned here refers to the linguistic division that happened when God confused the language at Babel. Even the Jewish historian Josephus (who lived near the time of Christ) stated, "He was called Peleg, because he was born at the dispersion of the nations to their various countries."[4]

Prominent modern theologians such as Dr. John Whitcomb reaffirm this as well.[5]

The Date

Returning to the discussion about the date, Archbishop Ussher's reckoning placed the date of Babel near 2242 BC.[6] See below for a comparison to other events according to Ussher.

Major Dates According to Ussher	
Major Event	Date
Creation	4004 BC
Global Flood	2348 BC
Tower of Babel	2242 BC
Call of Abraham	1921 BC
Time of the Judges (Moses was first)	1491 BC (God appeared to Moses in the burning bush)
Time of the Kings (Saul was first)	1095 BC
Split Kingdom	~975 BC
Christ Was Born	~5/4 BC

Ussher arrives at this date due to a historian named Manetho. Manetho claimed that the events at Babel occurred five years after the birth of Peleg. Is that right or wrong? We simply do not know. Manetho was not the best historian, as pointed out by a number of scholars today. I have seen dates of the scattering at 101 years after the flood (right when Peleg was born) and others near 130 years after the flood.[7]

One cannot help but notice this range. A significant number (120, to be precise) is within this range. Prior to the flood, because of the violence and sinful nature of man, God decreed a judgment of 120 years in Genesis 6:3.[8] This was essentially a countdown to the flood.

This number gives us an idea of the patience of God before judgment ensues. Considering that we are somewhere in the neighborhood of 120 years after God's declaration to be fruitful, multiply, and fill the earth, and though this is admittedly speculative, the timing makes sense.

Regardless, it was during the days of Peleg that the family groups left Babel in the plain of Shinar and traveled to different parts of the world, taking with them their own language that other families could not understand.[9] Not long after this, Babylon (2234 BC), Egypt (2188 BC), and Greece (2089 BC) began.[10] In a general sense, civilizations that were closer to Babel (e.g., those in the Middle East) were established prior to civilizations farther from Babel (e.g., those in Australia or the Americas). But this date for Babel seems to be consistent with what we find elsewhere.

An Objection

Some have objected and claimed that it took much longer to get enough people to build this huge tower. But there is an easy way to diffuse this argument. You can ask, "How many people are required to build a tower of unknown size?"

We simply do not know its height. Of course, it should have towered over the rest of the buildings in the area. The Bible says a tower "with its top in the heavens" (Genesis 11:4). There are nearly 30 ziggurats in the Mesopotamian area, none of which reach the stratosphere, but are instead just towers that merely reach over everything else. One might say that the name implies an immense height. But some names of the other ziggurat towers in that area have names that imply a link from earth to heaven:

1. Temple of the Stairway to Pure Heaven (Sippar)

2. Temple Which Links Heaven and Earth (Larsa)

Yet these towers are not skyscrapers by any means. Keep in mind that determined people can do things quickly when they put their minds to it. For example, in AD 1196, the soldiers of Richard the Lionheart built an immense castle (Chateau Gaillard) in Eure of Norman France. A small and yet impressive amount of the ruins remain to this day. What still fascinates researchers is the time it took to build this large, intricate structure . . . only about one year.[11] These workers then built an impressive church over the next four years, Saint Sauveur's Church.[12]

A rather simple and much smaller tower, like a ziggurat, would be no problem for a few determined families (no less than 78 families per the listing in Genesis 10) to build. These people in Genesis 11:1–9 were indeed working as one unit and had their minds set to build this structure. So they could surely put it up quickly; it would not have required centuries or even thousands of people. Josephus even commented on that:

> And they built a tower, neither sparing any pains, nor being in any degree negligent about the work; and by reason of the multitude of hands employed in it, it grew very high, sooner than anyone could expect; but the thickness of it was so great, and it was so strongly built, that thereby its great height seemed, upon the view, to be less than it really was.[13]

1 James Ussher, *The Annals of the World*, trans. Larry and Marion Pierce (Green Forest, AR: Master Books, 2003), p. 22.

2 The use of Ussher's dates are not an across-the-board endorsement of his work. We recognize that any human work contains errors; however, Ussher meticulously researched biblical and ancient history, and we are comfortable with using many of the dates he proposed.

3 Genesis 7:11—"In the six hundredth year of Noah's life, in the second month, on the seventeenth day of the month, on that day all the fountains of the great deep burst forth, and the windows of the heavens were opened."

4 William Whiston, *The Works of Josephus Complete and Unabridged* (Peabody, MA: Hendrickson Publishers, 1987), p. 37.

5 John Whitcomb, "Babel," *Creation*, June 2002, pp. 31–33, online at AnswersInGenesis.org/creation/v24/i3/babel.asp.

6 Ussher, *The Annals of the World*, p. 22.

7 This excludes those who hold to a gap theory between the flood and Babel, such as Dr. John Whitcomb, who places upwards of nearly 700–1,000 years between the flood and Babel. I have tremendous respect for Dr. Whitcomb, but humbly disagree.

8 Many people have mistakenly thought this referred to human longevity. However, for about 1,000 years after this, people still lived well beyond 120 years. Due to the context of the coming flood, it makes more sense to be in reference to the coming judgment; Genesis 6:3 says, "Then the LORD said, 'My Spirit shall not abide in man forever, for he is flesh: his days shall be 120 years.'"

9 This likely split apart knowledge, technology, music, history, and so on. I would leave open options that God permitted some individuals to have been granted the privilege of more than one language so that limited translation could occur between families, like father and son, and so that mass havoc did not completely ensue. There was a general trend for the directions of the three sons of Noah's descendants (Japheth—northeast and northwest; Ham—south and southwest; and Shem—Middle East, east, and southeast). Overall, this would still be within the class of "confusion" of languages. Perhaps Noah and his sons were given such a privilege to be able to speak with various descendants.

10 Larry Pierce, "In the Days of Peleg," *Creation*, December 1999, pp. 46–49.

11 "Chateau Gaillard," France This Way, francethisway.com/places/chateau-gaillard.php, see also: "Chateau Gaillard: The Stronghold of Richard the Lionheart," lesandelys.com/chateau-gaillard.

12 I have seen reports that it was 3,000 people involved in the project, and in some cases around 6,000 people. However, none of the references seemed solid enough to cite, so I chose to give the range here.

13 Flavius Josephus, *The Works of Flavius Josephus, Antiquity of the Jews*, chapter IV, trans. William Whiston (Grand Rapids, MI: Associated Publishers and Authors, Inc., year not given in print edition), p. 30.

Where Did the Scattering Occur?

Since the scattering was at Babel, which is between the Tigris and Euphrates Rivers, then was this near the garden of Eden? Some preliminary comments first.

Where Was the Garden of Eden?

In today's culture, people mistakenly think that the garden of Eden was in Iraq (the garden was actually destroyed by the flood), and yet Babel is in Iraq as well. Some think that these two places were nearby due to this misconception and due to the appearance of some names both pre-flood and post-flood.

To begin, the placement of the garden of Eden must be evaluated. If one jumps back to Genesis 2 and reads the description of the garden of Eden, there was one river that broke into four headwaters. The directions and places these rivers flow do not match at all with what we find today.

When we read Genesis 6–9, it is obvious that there was a global flood. A global flood would destroy any remnant of the garden of Eden; it would rearrange and pile up sediment so that the previous landscape, rivers and so on, would be utterly unrecognizable. But people mistake the garden of Eden in Iraq for good reason by asking, "So, if there was a global flood that destroyed everything, then why do the names of some places and features still exist?" Here are the most common examples:

Some Pre-flood and Post-flood References			
Name	Bible Reference Pre-flood	Bible Reference Post-flood	Person
Havilah	Genesis 2:11	Genesis 10:7, 29	Noah's grandson through Ham; Noah's great, great, great, great grandson through Shem
Cush	Genesis 2:13	Genesis 10:6	Noah's grandson through Ham
Asshur	Genesis 2:14	Genesis 10:22	Noah's grandson through Shem
Tigris	Genesis 2:14	Genesis 10:4	River in modern-day Iraq
Euphrates	Genesis 2:14	Genesis 15:18	River in modern-day Iraq

The answer to this conundrum is quite simple, but let's use some illustrations so that we can better understand this.

1. Names of places often transfer. For example, Versailles, Illinois, was named for Versailles, Kentucky, when settlers moved from Kentucky into Illinois. And before that, Versailles, Kentucky, was named for Versailles, France. If someone says, "Meet me in Versailles," you may have to ask, "Which one?" (There are other places that have a Versailles as well, such as Ohio and Indiana.)

2. Names of places often come from names of people. The land of Canaan was named for Noah's grandson Canaan. St. Louis, Missouri, was named for King Louis IX of France.

3. Names of people sometimes come from places. For example, London, the capital of the United Kingdom, is also a common name of numerous persons today.

Thus, names could easily have been transferred through the flood. Ham's grandson was likely named after the pre-flood land of Havilah. Cush was Ham's son, and Asshur was Shem's son, possibly named after the pre-flood land of Assyria. Noah, Ham, and Shem lived before the flood and would have remembered these regions. And, of course, these names have gone on to become names of regions where some of these people settled *after* the dispersal of the tower of Babel. Cush is modern-day Ethiopia.

For example, if I were to mention the Thames River, most people would quickly think of a river in southern England. However, the state of Connecticut in the US and Ontario, Canada, each have a river named Thames, too. When people settled in the Americas from Europe, they named some rivers for rivers they were familiar with. Why would we expect Noah and his descendants to do any differently? The Tigris and Euphrates that we know today in modern-day Iraq were named for the famous headwaters in the garden of Eden.

There is no contradiction but merely a situation of naming new places, rivers, and people with previously used names.

Where Was the Tower of Babel Located? Was It in the Region of Iraq?

The scattering took place at Babel . . . but where exactly is that? The Bible describes it as the plain of Shinar in Genesis 11:2. They were moving from the east.[1] This is in reference to where Noah came off of the ark and had settled to become a farmer (Genesis 9).

Did Noah Leave the Ark Site?

In Genesis 9, we read the account of Ham's sinful actions toward Noah and the subsequent curse to Canaan, Ham's youngest son, who was likely much like Ham but worse.

Furthermore, Noah knew better than to curse Ham, whom God had blessed in Genesis 9:1 when they came off of the ark.

At the time of these events, Noah likely settled with most of his descendants. So this westerly movement of people (Genesis 11:2) refers to their migration from where they had settled with Noah.[2]

Some researchers have suggested the migration was west-ward from the landing site of the ark.[3] However, Noah had the pick of the world in which to settle and had no reason to set up housekeeping beside the ark. Furthermore, to become a farmer, Noah would not have selected the rocky soil on the mountains of Ararat.

Noah was living in a tent (not the large wooden structure of the ark) because the Lord said to come off the ark and fill the earth. Noah had listened to God before the flood, so we would expect him to obey God here. Therefore, the starting point for this migration would not have been the ark's landing site but where Noah had settled and become a farmer.

Shinar and Babel

As the descendants of Noah traveled westward, they found a plain in the land of Shinar and settled there. *Shinar* literally means "between two rivers." This would place them between the only two parallel rivers in the whole area. That is between the Tigris and Euphrates Rivers. They would naturally name the rivers near which they settled for pre-flood rivers. *Shinar* occurs eight times in the Old Testament:

> The beginning of his kingdom was Babel, Erech, Accad, and Calneh, in the land of *Shinar*. (Genesis 10:10)

And as people migrated from the east, they found a plain in the land of *Shinar* and settled there. (Genesis 11:2)

In the days of Amraphel king of *Shinar*, Arioch king of Ellasar, Chedorlaomer king of Elam, and Tidal king of Goiim. (Genesis 14:1)

With Chedorlaomer king of Elam, Tidal king of Goiim, Amraphel king of *Shinar*, and Arioch king of Ellasar, four kings against five. (Genesis 14:9)

When I saw among the spoil a beautiful cloak from *Shinar*, and 200 shekels of silver, and a bar of gold weighing 50 shekels, then I coveted them and took them. And see, they are hidden in the earth inside my tent, with the silver underneath. (Joshua 7:21)

In that day the Lord will extend his hand yet a second time to recover the remnant that remains of his people, from Assyria, from Egypt, from Pathros, from Cush, from Elam, from *Shinar*, from Hamath, and from the coastlands of the sea. (Isaiah 11:11)

And the Lord gave Jehoiakim king of Judah into his hand, with some of the vessels of the house of God. And he brought them to the land of *Shinar*, to the house of his god, and placed the vessels in the treasury of his god. (Daniel 1:2)

He said to me, "To the land of *Shinar*, to build a house for it. And when this is prepared, they will set the basket down there on its base." (Zechariah 5:11)

These definitive references make it clear that the Israelites knew the location of Shinar. Shinar was the region known as Babylonia or Chaldea in southern Mesopotamia. Later, because of their persistent disobedience, God allowed the Assyrian Empire, and later Babylonian Empire, to conquer the divided kingdoms of the Israelites, and many of the people were deported to a region they knew as Shinar. This was the time of Daniel, Shadrach, Meshach, and Abednego to give you an idea of this later empire.

The region of Mesopotamia (Babylon, modern Iraq today) was home to a number of powerful empires in the past, particularly Assyria, Babylon, and Persia.

Interestingly, the word for Babel and Babylon is the same in Hebrew. This Hebrew word is translated twice in Genesis 10–11 as "Babel" and elsewhere translated as "Babylon." The "Babel" translation is likely chosen to distinguish the former from the latter empire. *The Theological Wordbook of the Old Testament* explains the Hebrew word *babel* as follows:

> Babylon is the Greek spelling of the name which in Hebrew is uniformly "Babel." The word [*sic*] occurs some 290 times and refers to an ancient city on the eastern bank of the Euphrates about twenty miles south of Bagdad, near the modern village of Hilla in Iraq.[4]

TOWER OF BABEL

IRAQ ★ TOWER OF BABEL

possible location

Babel and Babylon are indeed the same place by the biblical accounts and can be found on maps even in the present time. This is the most probable place where the events of the tower occurred.[5] Subsequently, a later empire was built.

---

1 The Hebrew word for *east* could also be translated "eastward," but most translators believe this to be "from the east" as opposed to "toward the east."

2 The Hebrew word translated as "from the east" in Genesis 11:2 can mean either "eastward" or "from the east." This makes it difficult to understand the exact location. What we can say for sure is that Noah's farm was primarily east or west from Babel and the land of Shinar.

3 Anne Habermehl, "Where in the World Is the Tower of Babel?" *Answers Research Journal* 4 (2011): 25–53; Anne Habermehl, "A Review of the Search for Noah's Ark," in Andrew Snelling, ed., *Proceedings of the Sixth International Conference of Creationism* (Pittsburgh, PA; Dallas, TX: Creation Science Fellowship; Institute for Creation Research, 2008), pp. 485–502.

4 *Theological Wordbook of the Old Testament,* eds. R. Laird Harris, Gleason L. Archer, and Bruce K. Waltke (Chicago, IL: Moody Bible Institute, 1980), s.v. לבב.

5 I would leave open a slim possibility that the original tower itself was not in the city but was nearby, but the text of Scripture seemed to equate these two places (Babel and Babylon) without further discussion.

Was the Tower of Babel Built or Not?

Special thanks to Hebraist Dr. Russell Fuller for his comments on this topic.

Illustrations of the tower of Babel range from a completed ziggurat to a partially completed structure to a simple foundation! Why the discrepancy?

According to most translations, the tower of Babel *was built*, according to (Genesis 11:5), and it was the *city* that they stopped building (Genesis 11:8). Though the LXX Greek translation adds in that *the tower ceased to be built* as well, this is done without any Hebrew textual basis. A handful of translations say "building" instead of "built" or "builded," likely for this reason.

Some have thought that the Hebrew wording does not mean it was built, but the word for built/building is *banah/baanuw* and is used in a perfect tense. If the tower was built, this is how it would be stated in Hebrew. Even today, we call a built building a "building" today.

Commentators Keil and Delitzch, believing it was built significantly but not entirely in their Old Testament commentary, say of this word usage in Genesis 11:5 that "the perfect *baanuw* refers to the building as one finished up to a certain point." So the question is how complete? Perhaps some finishing touches were necessary. But for the most part, it was complete. The tower was not merely a foundation. And so this may be an option, though this author is not entirely convinced.

If one argued that the tower was not built to any significant degree, then that person would have to argue that hosts of structures in the Old Testament were also not built, such as the temple (e.g., 1 Kings 10:4), many houses (e.g., 1 Kings 9:24), many cities (e.g., Numbers 32:37–38), and so on, since they all use this same Hebrew word in a perfect tense.

Furthermore, *banah* in this verse is used not just in reference to the tower but also the city. If we were to argue the tower was not built, then we would have to argue that the city was not really built either. The fact that the Bible calls it a "tower" should be sufficient to believe it was a tower and not the mere beginnings of a structure. And the fact that the Bible clarifies in Genesis 11:8 that they left off building the *city* should warrant that the tower didn't really need further work.

The LXX (also known as the Septuagint, a Greek translation of the Hebrew Scriptures completed about 200–250 years before Christ) added the word *tower* to Genesis 11:8 in their translation without biblical warrant, and this has likely been the main reason some still think the tower was only partially built.

The LXX is good in many places, but it is not considered a good translation in Genesis, as it distorts the ages of the patriarchs (e.g., Noah's grandfather Methuselah would be living over a decade after the flood without being on the ark); mistranslates "*sons*" as angels in Genesis 6:2 (6:3 by the LXX's reckoning in the *Codex Alexadrinus* and some Vaticanus texts); mixes the Greek philosophy of the day by having a solid dome to translate expanse (*raqiya*) as something solid and firm[1]; and so on. The standard Hebrew Masoretic text makes it clear that it was not the tower but the city that ceased to be built if any clarification was needed.

Some argue that Genesis 11:6 ("and this is only the beginning of what they will do") refers to the tower. But it makes more sense that the Lord is referring to their sinful intention of defying his command to fill the post-flood world, given in Genesis 9:1 and 9:7. In other words, they were building the city and tower in defiance of God's command. A city or a tower is not inherently evil, but disobedience to God's command is.

Archaeology may provide a good confirmation of this line of reasoning. The oldest recorded image of the tower of Babel, found in the *The Schøyen Collection, MS 2063*, is an inscribed stele with Nebuchadnezzar II and the image of a virtually complete tower.[2]

Nebuchadnezzar II was the king of Babylon, the later empire that flourished when Israel and Judah were in captivity. This was the time of Daniel and Jeremiah, about 600 BC for a biblical reference.

Tower of Babel Stele with Nebuchadnezzar II

In this image, the tower is essentially complete, with only a small portion at the very top that is slightly indiscernible. But the tower is basically complete, though one should still be tentative rather than dogmatic. But in the grand scheme, it was complete enough to serve the function it was intended to do, which was to keep people from scattering.

Nebuchadnezzar II wanted to tear down this rather old and dilapidated tower (even in his day) and rebuild it. Of course, Nebuchadnezzar II did not have this opportunity. A Greek historian named Herodotus commented on it in his day when he was in Babylon:

> The temple of Bêl, the Babylonian Zeus [...] was still in existence in my time. It has a solid central tower, one stadium square, with a second erected on top of it and then a third, and so on up to eight. All eight towers can be climbed by a spiral way running round the outside, and about half way up there are seats for those who make the ascent to rest on. On the summit of the topmost tower stands a great temple with a fine large couch in it, richly covered, and a golden table beside it. The shrine contains no image, and no one spends the night there except (if we may believe that Chaldaeans who are the priests of Bêl) one Babylonian woman, all alone, whoever it may be that the god has chosen. The Chaldaeans also say—though I do not believe them—that the god enters the temple in person and takes his rest upon the bed.[3]

Later, Alexander the Great had it torn down with the same idea to rebuild it, but his death at a young age prevented it from ever being rebuilt. And so it passed into pages of history.

---

1   Many Greeks believed the heavens were basically solid, and this influenced these translators to say the expanse was something solid. This has affected numerous translations since then as the Latin version (Jerome's Vulgate) then translated this as something firm, and the KJV and NKJV translators followed suit with a firmament.

2   Rossella Lorenzi, "Ancient Texts Part of Earliest Known Documents," Discovery News, news.discovery.com/history/tower-of-babel-111227.html.

3   Herodotus, *Histories* 1.181–2; available online at livius.org/he-hg/herodotus/logoi.html.

What Was the Purpose of the Tower of Babel?

Even though the Bible records the general reason the tower was built, people have suggested a number of additional specific reasons. These need to be evaluated.

To Survive Another Global Flood?

Let's first see what respected Jewish historian Josephus suggested. He wrote, "For that he would build a tower too high for the waters to be able to reach."[1]

Josephus commented that the tower was built in order to survive another flood—to escape any such repeat judgment from God. But if that were the case, why build it in a flood plain? The plain of Shinar flooded regularly, though measures have been taken to reduce that today.

Also, this neglects the promise of God not to send a flood to destroy all life as he had previously stated (Genesis 8:21, 9:11, 9:15; Psalm 104:9).[2,3,4,5] (Of course, the people were ignoring God's command, so it would not be out of character for them to also ignore his promise.)

Dr. John Gill, a leading Baptist expositor and Hebraist of the 1700s, commented

> It is generally thought what led them to it was to secure them from another flood, they might be in fear of; but this seems not likely, since they had the covenant and oath of God, that the earth should never be destroyed by water any more; and besides, had this been the thing in view, they would not have chosen a plain to build on, a plain that lay between two of the greatest rivers, Tigris, and Euphrates, but rather one of the highest mountains and

hills they could have found: nor could a building of brick be a sufficient defense against such a force of water, as the waters of the flood were; and besides, but few at most could be preserved at the top of the tower, to which, in such a case, they would have betook themselves.[6]

Dr. Gill rightly points out the problems with this view.

Idolatry?

One idea was that the tower was built for idolatry like a temple to the sun for worship. This may be problematic since the Babel builders clearly knew God's command to fill the earth. Their intentional defiance was going against this command in Genesis 11:4. If they knew the command, they likely knew *who* gave it. So it makes sense they still retained knowledge of God, even if this event marked the beginning of rebellion from God post-flood.

Though with rebellion, this could occur. When people turn their back on God, it does not take long to start deviating in many areas, including idolatry.

Fame?

Some suggest that the tower was built to spread their fame far and wide. And this may well be one of the reasons since they were doing this to make a name for themselves (Genesis 11:4).

However, if people were concentrated there, then far and wide was not much. Perhaps their fame was meant to be an "enduring fame" to make a name for themselves for greatness in subsequent generations.

Astronomical Observations and Worshipping the Heavens?

Some have thought the tower was used to stargaze, which was the basis for marking seasons and years as commanded in Genesis 1:14.[7] This may well have been one of the reasons for it.

Towers and temples across the globe were used for such things as timekeeping. It is easy to see when people neglect God; the descendants of Noah start to look for other things to worship. So it is possible that such things helped prompt the patriarchs to serve false gods.

Many temples and structures in the ancient world were used for mapping the heavens and telling time through astronomical observations, such as the following:

- South American Incan temples of the sun and moon
- Indian Mnajdra temples
- Mesoamerican Alta Vista's Labyrinth or Pyramid of the Sun in Mexico
- Stonehenge (marks solar and lunar observations)

Many of these ancient structures could have been used for such a purpose. But this would not necessarily be a reason for keeping people from scattering.

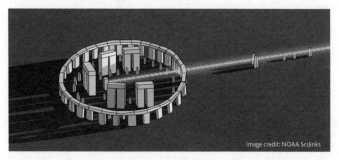

Image credit: NOAA SciJinks

Sacrifice?

Although the tower of Babel long preceded the Levitical laws concerning ceremonial sacrifice, we know from the Genesis record of Abel's and Noah's sacrifices that people understood sacrifice as a part of worship.

God had not given any instructions concerning a central place of sacrifice in his recorded Word. On the contrary, he had commanded people to scatter. However, if the people in unison designated the tower as the official place for sacrifice, then people could not travel too far. Such an edifice would be used for a supposedly godly purpose and yet be in defiance of God's Word. Recall Saul when he offered a sacrifice, claimed to be godly, and yet was defying God's Word (1 Samuel 15:20–22).[8] It is better to obey than sacrifice. Many towers around the world were used for sacrifice—sadly, even human sacrifice.

Burial?

Was it a place of burial, as was the case with some ziggurats and pyramids, such as many in Egypt? It is possible. However, the first recorded death of anyone after the flood was Peleg based on the dates of overlap (Genesis 11:19), and yet the scattering from the tower occurred in the days of Peleg. Could the tower have been a burial place for Noah's wife (who seems obviously to be missing in the account of Genesis 9:18–29), a son, or a daughter-in-law? The Bible does not address this question.

What We Know

What we know for sure is that the tower's primary purpose was to keep people from scattering and to make a name for themselves. And it obviously served that purpose because the Lord had to intervene to confuse the languages to make people scatter.

Some may think that the building project itself was what kept people from scattering and was not related to any other underlying purpose. However, this is problematic.

If the construction project was what kept people from scattering (i.e., merely building a tower), then upon completion the people should have naturally scattered. There would have been no need for a confusion of languages on God's part (he knows all things). But God's intervention *was necessary*. So it was not merely building the tower that kept people around, but the tower did indeed have an underlying purpose.

---

1 Revised Works of Josephus, chapter 4, Tower of Babel—Confusion of Tongues. 2242 BC, line 114.

2 Genesis 8:21—And when the LORD smelled the pleasing aroma, the LORD said in his heart, "I will never again curse the ground because of man, for the intention of man's heart is evil from his youth. Neither will I ever again strike down every living creature as I have done."

3 Genesis 9:11—I establish my covenant with you, that never again shall all flesh be cut off by the waters of the flood, and never again shall there be a flood to destroy the earth.

4 Genesis 9:15—I will remember my covenant that is between me and you and every living creature of all flesh. And the waters shall never again become a flood to destroy all flesh.

5 Psalm 104:9—You set a boundary that they may not pass, so that they might not again cover the earth.

6 John Gill, *Commentary on the Whole Bible*, notes on Genesis 11:4; available online at biblestudytools. com/commentaries/gills-exposition-of-the-bible/genesis-11-4.html.

7 Genesis 1:14—And God said, "Let there be lights in the expanse of the heavens to separate the day from the night. And let them be for signs and for seasons, and for days and years."

8 1 Samuel 15:20–22—And Saul said to Samuel, "I have obeyed the voice of the LORD. I have gone on the mission on which the LORD sent me. I have brought Agag the king of Amalek, and I have devoted the Amalekites to destruction. But the people took of the spoil, sheep and oxen, the best of the things devoted to destruction, to sacrifice to the LORD your God in Gilgal." And Samuel said, "Has the LORD as great delight in burnt offerings and sacrifices, as in obeying the voice of the LORD? Behold, to obey is better than sacrifice, and to listen than the fat of rams."

What Did the Tower Look Like?

In a previous chapter, we saw an ancient stele that had a depiction of the tower of Babel on it. It was a ziggurat in form. Is that accurate? After all, we see some popular artwork that has the tower of Babel rounded. What is the truth?

If we jump back to about 400 years ago to an illustration in the King James Version (KJV) of 1611, we find this rounded image in the pages prior to the biblical text (see bottom left).

Even before this in 1547, Cornelis Anthonisz from Amsterdam did an etching of a rounded tower being destroyed by God (see bottom right).

KJV, 1611   Cornelis Anthonisz, 1547

From 1563, there is Pieter Bruegel's famed painting:

Pieter Bruegel, 1563

We also find a painting about this same time by Lucas van Valckenborch in 1568:

Lucas van Valckenborch, 1568

Even in more modern times, we find rounded images following these previous examples. One of the more famous ones, by Gustave Dore, was completed the same year that the American Civil War ended.

Gustave Dore, 1865

These images are beautiful, but they may not be the most accurate. I find that, in some instances, they play into the false assumption that the tower of Babel reached very high in the atmosphere, like the stratosphere, with clouds encircling the top. In each case, they are a rounded tower where one can access it by walking along the outside at a particular grade. However, not all them wind in the same direction.

To informed researchers, the tower of Babel is most likely a type of ziggurat, although the Bible does not give specific dimensions. The Hebrew word for *tower* used in Genesis 11, referring to the tower of Babel, is *migdal*—by analogy, a rostrum; figuratively, a (pyramidal) bed of flowers.[1]

Interestingly, this word means "tower" but figuratively reflects a flowerbed that yields a pyramidal shape. This gives a little support to the idea that the tower of Babel may have been pyramidal or ziggurat-shaped. In fact, there are many ziggurats found around the world, and around 30 are in the Mesopotamian area. John Walton of the Associates for Biblical Research, an archaeology group, says:

> To call the ziggurat a tower is not inaccurate, and as a matter of fact, the term they used is derived from the Hebrew term *gdl* (to be large), which is somewhat parallel to the etymological root of the Akkadian word, *ziqqurat* (zaqaru, to be high). Despite the fact then that the Hebrew term is used primarily in military senses or as watch towers, the context here and the known background of the narrative prevent us from being limited to that semantic range.[2]

One famous tower is a ziggurat at Ur (The Great Ziggurat at Ur) with a reconstruction by excavator Sir Leonard Woolley. It was buried and in ruins, and after excavations, it was

still impressive, yet missing its upper parts.

Dr. Clifford Wilson, a popular, world-renowned archeologist, in a study on Babel and the archaeology thereof, suggested this foundation as the possible site in Babylon as the remains of the tower's foundation (see right).[3]

If this is truly the foundation, then clearly it was square in shape, like other ziggurats. This is what would be expected from the tower of Babel stele.

In what is now Iraq, Robert Koldewey excavated a structure some think to be the foundation of the original tower of Babel. It underlays a later ziggurat that was thought to be built or restored by Hammurabi in the 19th century BC.[4]

Even the Tyndale Bible Dictionary reveals:

> The first ziggurat at Babylon was built by Shar-kali-sharri, king of Akkad in the latter part of the 23rd century BC. Archaeologists understand that this ziggurat was destroyed and rebuilt several times across the centuries. It apparently lay in ruins from sometime around 2000 BC to around 1830 BC, at which time a forebear of Hammurabi (1728–1636 BC) founded or rebuilt the city named Bab-ilu, or Babel.[5]

The New Bible Dictionary also affirms this:

> The ziggurat at Babylon was demolished by Xerxes in 472 BC, and though Alexander cleared the rubble prior to its restoration this was thwarted by his death. The bricks were subsequently removed by the local inhabitants, and today the site of Etemenanki is a pit (Es-Saḥn) as deep as the original construction was high.[6]

This is the likely place of the original tower, but will we ever be absolutely certain about its exact location? I leave this open for debate. The late archaeologist Dr. Clifford Wilson affirms this as the potential site of the tower of Babel.[7]

Regardless, when people were scattered from Babel in the days of Peleg, they likely took this building concept with them to places all over the world. It makes sense that many of the families that were scattered from Babel took varying ideas of the tower to their new lands and began building projects of their own. It is highly possible that they even came up with newer and better designs and materials for their specified towers (e.g., cut stone instead of baked bricks and so on).

Ziggurats, pyramids, mounds, and the like have been found in many parts of the world—from Mesopotamia to Egypt to South America. Among the earliest structures in Egypt was a step pyramid, which is a ziggurat. The ancient Chinese built pyramids and the Mississippian culture built mounds. Pyramids are classed slightly differently from ziggurats, as are mounds, but the similarities are striking.

Ziggurats and pyramids all over the world are an excellent confirmation of the original recorded in God's Word—the tower of Babel.

1 Strong's Hebrew Lexicon, Online Bible, Larry Pierce, 2012.

2 John Walton, "Is There Archaeological Evidence for the Tower of Babel?" Associates for Biblical Research, biblearchaeology.org/post/2008/05/Is-there-Archaeological-Evidence-for-the-Tower-of-Babel.aspx.

3 Clifford Wilson, *The Bible Comes Alive* (Green Forest, Ark.: New Leaf Press, 1997), p. 47.

4 David Down, "Ziggurats in the News," *Archaeological Diggings*, March–April 2007, pp. 3–7.

5 *Tyndale Bible Dictionary*, eds. Walter A. Elwell and Philip Wesley Comfort (Wheaton, Ill.: Tyndale House Publishers, 2001), S. 137.

6 D. R. W. Wood, *New Bible Dictionary* (InterVarsity Press, 1996, c1982, c1962), S. 109.

7 Clifford Wilson, Visual Highlights of the Bible, Volume 1, *From Creation to Abraham* (Boronia, Victoria, Australia: Pacific Christian Ministries, 1993), pp. 50–51.

Did All ~7,000 Languages Today Come Out of Babel?

Introduction

The tower of Babel explains why everyone does not speak the same language today.

There are over 6,900 spoken languages in the world today.[1] Were there that many people who came out of Babel with a new language? Not at all. So how do we explain this?

Believe it or not, creationists and evolutionists actually agree on something here. We agree that languages change. Of course, the evolutionary view assumes that we all go back to one single grunting "ape" language or "proto-language." Naturally, this is in opposition to what God says in Genesis 11:1–9, where God is the originator of the first language and confused that language due to rebellion at Babel.

Variations Within Language Families

But languages change over time. Let's look at changes in the English language as an example. As a United States citizen who grew up in the United States, I speak American English. But, to be more precise, when I return home to my family, I speak a Western Illinois dialect that sounds like a choppy-county style that is rather conversational; some even denote this as "hick." Yes, I admit it! Though I am proud of my humble dialect, many others find it rather unsophisticated and difficult to listen to.

In various parts of the United States, American English is quite varied. From the New England states to the Midwest to the West Coast, there is indeed some variation. Need I mention Tennessee, whose residents have a unique variety of English all to themselves—but unlike my dialect, many agree that Tennessean is actually quite pleasant to listen to!

But these varieties of American English are quite different from English around the world. British English varies from Canadian English, which varies from Indian (subcontinent) English, which varies from Australian and New Zealand English. Let's face it, English has variations today, and it continues changing every year!

If we jump back, English has changed so much over the course of 1,000 years that early speakers would hardly recognize it today and vice versa. Take a look at the changes in Matthew 6:9 over the course of about 1,000 years (this does not take into account accents and shifting in sounds).

Beginning of Matthew 6:9	Date
Our Father who art in heaven and/or Our Father who is in heaven	Late Modern English (1700s)
Our father which art in heauen	Early Modern English (1500–1700) (KJV 1611)
Oure fader that art in heuenis	Middle English (1100–1500)
Fæder ure þu þe eart on heofonum	Old English (c. 1000 AD)

One thousand years ago, English looked somewhat German. But to make things worse, English is actually classed as a Germanic language along with languages like Swedish, German, Norwegian, Dutch, Afrikaans, Austrian, Icelandic, and so on. It was Germanic tribes that brought this language to the British Isles (via the Angles—which is where we get the name *English*—and Saxons primarily).[2]

But English began changing from other forms of Germanic when the French/Latin-based language was introduced to the British Isles when the Normans (who spoke a French/Latin-based language) conquered England in AD 1066. English began borrowing many French and Latin terms and the languages began to mix. This is actually a rather common event between nations that are conquered—they assimilate cultural and language aspects. This is likely why Germanic Angles' language on the British Isles deviated from mainland Germanic languages. The Germanic that the Angles and Saxons spoke assimilated with the other languages spoken by the tribes on the Isles (Welch, Scots, Irish, etc.) even before the Norman Conquest.

Just as English has changed significantly over the past 1,000 years, it becomes easy to see how the original languages, such as an original Germanic language family at Babel, could have rapidly changed in the 4,000 years since that time, whether spoken or written.

From a big picture, the number of languages that came out of Babel would have been far less than the language divisions we have today. In other words, several languages today comprise a single language family.

Root Languages from Babel Are "in the Ballpark" of Language Families Today

So where did all these languages come from? Linguists recognize that most languages have similarities to other languages. Related languages belong to what are called *language families*. These original language families resulted from God's confusion of the language at Babel. Since that time, the original language families have grown and changed into the abundant number of languages today.

Noah's great, great grandson Eber fathered Peleg when the events at Babel took place. The language of the Old Testament (with the exception of the Aramaic bits)[3] we know of as Hebrew is named after Eber (think "Eberew" or Hebrew). The Bible lists Noah's grandsons, great grandsons, great-great grandsons, and great-great-great grandsons who received a language at Babel in Genesis 10. Eber was one!

Out of Eber, languages like Hebrew (through Isaac), Arabic (through Joktan and later dominated by Ishmael and other sons of Abraham),[4] the Ammonite language (through Lot and his son Ben-Ammi), the Moabite language (through Lot and his son Moab), and so on came.[5]

From Japheth (Genesis 10:2–5), there came 14 language families; from Ham (Genesis 10:6–20), there came 39; from Shem (Genesis 10:22–31), there came at least 25 (excluding Peleg and other children who may have just been born).

The total minimum number of languages that may have come out of Babel according to Genesis 10 may have been at least 78, assuming Noah, Ham, Shem, Japheth, and Peleg did not receive a new language. This excludes some descendants of Shem who are given slight mention in Genesis 11:11–17; they may have also received a language.

Both *Vistawide World Languages and Cultures*[6] and *Ethnologue*,[7] companies that provide statistics on languages, agree that there are more than 78 (estimates constantly change but are currently sitting between 94 and 120 languages families). Some groupings include sign languages and constructed languages that have been developed. With further study in years to come, this may change to a smaller number, but this figure is well within the range of families that dispersed from Babel (Genesis 10).

More on Languages

One thing we can learn from history about languages was given previously, but I want to draw out some important points. Specifically, I want to discuss the issue of Arabic originally being a language of Joktan but becoming dominated by Abraham's and his progeny. Historians like James Anderson and Josephus have pointed out that Ishmael and Abraham's other sons with Keturah dominated the Arabian Peninsula (as well as other places in the Middle East and North Africa). We even have a lineage from Ishmael to Muhammad, who conquered much of the Middle East and North Africa and forced them into a counterfeit of Christianity called Mohammedism or Islam. This took place much later (after AD 600), but continues to affect the languages in these areas.[8]

Language Changes

When we look at Arabic today, it is very similar to biblical Hebrew. The reason is simply that Ishmael spoke Hebrew due to his father, Abraham, who was also a Hebrew (Genesis 14:13). So as he dominated the lands on the Arabian Peninsula, so did his variant form of Hebrew. Furthermore, many of Abraham's other sons with Keturah also settled in Arabia, adding to this language becoming dominant among the Arabs.

This also happened with Aramaic (spoken by descendants of Aram) and Phoenician (spoken by some Canaanites) in or near the land of Canaan. These lands were basically conquered or heavily influenced by the Israelites who spoke Hebrew. So although Aramaic was originally connected with Aram and his language family, the long history of Israelites speaking a form of Hebrew dominated their lands. Sometimes the languages mix but have more elements of one compared to another. Even Hebrew has

Egyptian, Aramaic, Canaanite, Babylonian, and other borrowed words. This is expected since Abraham and his progeny lived among many of these peoples.

Consider the case with English. We still retain more German roots in our language, even though we have much French and Latin influence. Although English dominates the UK and Ireland, the languages mixed with previous languages that were already on the island. This helps distinguish English from other Germanic-based languages. Rome, speaking Latin, dominated Spain, Portugal, France, and many other places with their language. This is a common trend.

These are basic examples; it gets more complicated. (More information on some of the migrations of people can be found in chapter 17 of *Tower of Babel*, which covers where people groups went and how many languages have mixed, been lost, or had something similar happen . . . sometimes repeatedly.)

Constructed Languages

Another aspect of languages is the creativity of man. We are made in the image of God after all. If God can create languages, why can't man make them up? In fact, we have! For those who are familiar with the popular television show *Star Trek*, there was a make-believe language in that show called "Klingon" based on a mythical group of beings called Klingons. So what happened? A creative person named Marc Okrand came up with the language for use on the show and developed it into a full-fledged language. And people have now learned it and can communicate using it!

This is not the first time something like this has happened. These are called "constructed languages," or *planned*, or *artificial* languages. Perhaps the most famous example of this is Esperanto, which is now an international language with native speakers born into it.

But computer programmers have developed languages to work within computers (Fortran, Basic, "C", HTML, and so on). Many times there are code systems, which are like a type of encoded language used in war. There is Morse code and sign languages. Even I developed a written code language that I have been able to readily read and write since grade school! The creativity of man could indeed accelerate the issue of languages since the time of Babel.

Language Isolates

There are many languages that have no relationship to any language family that we know of. They are called language "isolates."

Evolutionary presuppositions may be at fault for the classification of some of these. In North America, they assume primitive native man came basically via one route across the Bering Sea land bridge when it was open (due to an ice age)[9], and so all the languages should match up in North and South America. When they do not match up, they usually default to an isolate language. I would suggest these isolates be compared more closely with languages in other parts of the world before we make them definitive isolates. They could be related to language families that came out of Babel where some of the descendants who spoke that language settled in various parts of the world—including the Americas.

Christians often point out that there were early seafaring people (Genesis 10:5) who could have made it to the Americas by boat, bringing a multitude of language families to the Americas. So some isolates may reflect similarities to certain language families in other parts of the world.

But we should also consider the constructed language approach. Some may well be isolates or constructed languages. When people are left to themselves, they have likely automatically lost a big portion of the words from their root languages (it is rare for someone to know *all* the words of their language). From there, people come up with new words and continue to lose old words in subsequent generations. We do this in English too—we add new words yearly (e.g., *ain't*) and forget many words have mostly fallen into disuse (e.g., *groovy* or *sibilation*). Given some time, be it decades or centuries, an isolated group can develop almost an entirely new language.

A Proto-language?

In an evolutionary framework, the concept is that language slowly developed among evolving humans and originated with a "proto-language" or the ancestor to all languages. This language was supposedly "primitive" (think "primate-like"). It was surely based on grunts and other basic animal sounds since people were supposed to be animals.

The claim is that the first proto-language came about nearly two million years ago with *Homo erectus*.[10] *Homo erectus* is a name evolutionists have given to a group of humans. Of course, this is purely a guess based on the story of evolution and millions of years. Christians should beware of humanistic ideas like this and the arbitrariness behind them. But researchers are trying to find commonalities, especially with grammar, and have produced various models. One such model is called "universal grammar" or UG. It still falls short, as many researchers note, rightly recognizing that with the diversity of languages and so many exceptions, such an effort to reconstruct a universal grammar may not only be improbable but perhaps impossible.[11]

One must understand that the secular humanistic community *must* have a story in place to make sense of languages (speech, written, and sign). It was like this with the old Greek mythologies; they needed to have stories to explain why the sun took a particular path in the sky. In the same way, evolutionary storytelling is a necessity when looking at real issues like language.

We can speak simply because the Creator made us in his image to communicate with him. We can think, reason, and be creative in ways animals simply never could. But an unbelieving secular community has refused to allow God in the door. So they must come up with stories to try to explain language. And so they appeal to animals (because they believe we are simply animals) for answers.

Due to evolutionary presuppositions, they assume that man evolved from ape-like ancestors, so apes today should be the closest things to us and hence to human language. This brings us to studies on apes like Koko, who was able to learn certain signs.

Koko and Other Animals to the Rescue?

Koko is a fascinating gorilla but is far from being human. Koko has learned nearly 1,000 signs in American Sign Language, and Koko knows quite a number of voice commands. It has taken Koko nearly 32 years to learn all this.[12] And other animals like the bonobo named Kanzi have also been trained to hear commands.[13]

These trained responses are similar to that of dogs and many other animals. They can be trained to do or respond to certain sounds or motions and even give a response in return. For example, the world's smartest dog according to *Guinness Book of World Records*, Chandra Leah, can recognize over 1,022 commands and responds to each accordingly—some are even math problems! Many of these commands are vocal or hand signals, much like the commands Koko is given.[14]

Yet Chandra Leah, being only 10 years old, is much younger than Koko, and many dogs have this capability, so dogs seem to be a far superior specimen than the alleged apes that are supposedly our closest relatives. Trained response, however, is much different than the ability to use reasoning in the same manner as humans.

Man is made in the image of God; animals are not.[15] This is an extreme difference and why looking to animal behavior for answers will never reveal the truth about human origins or human language—one should stick with what God says.

Conclusion

From a biblical perspective, is it feasible for 7,000 languages to develop from about a minimum of 78 root languages in 4,000 years? No problem!

The languages that came out of the confusion at Babel were "root languages" or language families. Over time, those root languages have varied: borrowing from other languages, developing new terms, phrases, and pronunciations, losing older words and phrases, and, just like Germanic languages, have variations even in the ones known specifically as American English.

But notice the contrast in the secular view, where we all allegedly evolved from rudimentary ancestors with a single primitive grunting language. This theoretical "proto-language" is not even close to the multitude of root languages that gave rise to languages of today. It is good to be Christian today, understanding languages from a biblical perspective instead of the world's faulty ideas.

But let's clarify a misconception. God is responsible for the languages and it was due to judgment . . . so is having one language a bad thing? Philo, an early Jewish historian, hit the nail on the head when he said, "For it was not the languages which were the causes of men's uniting for evil objects, but the emulation and rivalry of their souls in wrong-doing."[16]

And consider what the Apostle Paul says about languages:

> There are doubtless many different languages in the world, and none is without meaning. (1 Corinthians 14:10)

Postscript: An Ancient Chinese Language

Let's look at the significance of ancient Chinese characters. Researchers like Dr. Ethel Nelson, Dr. Ginger Tong Chock, and Richard Broadberry have published extensively on the significance of this particular language dialect.

Recall how some languages are built on images (more graphic in style). Many Chinese languages and dialects (and other oriental languages) are like this. English is different in that we use symbols to represent sounds that we arrange into words and sentences. But these ancient Chinese characters, being built on graphics, mean something, and this makes it easier to "see" some significance.

Many of the characters are built directly on Genesis. The character for "boat" was made of up three other characters—a vessel, eight, and mouth. Interestingly, in Genesis 6–8, the ark was a large vessel that had eight people aboard and only eight human mouths to speak and feed. The name of the one true God that the Chinese originally worshipped and sacrificed to was named ShangDi (some transliterate this as ShangTi). The characters for ShangDi are the character for "emperor" and "above/heavenly."[17] These are just some small nuggets. There is much more that has been documented, and I suggest researching this in more detail.[18]

This language is fascinating. Was the written form of this language developed by men as they left or settled later on? Or was it part of the written language that God instituted at Babel? We may never know, but there is no doubt the significance of the characters of ancient Chinese.

Does such significance abound in other languages? According to 1 Corinthians 14:10, it may. For each language conveys meaning in what is spoken and received (e.g., information), and that in itself is significant. Will we ever know any extra significance in other languages? Only further research will one day be able to answer that.

1   Vistawide, "World Language Families," vistawide.com/languages/language_families_statistics1.htm.

2   There were Germanic tribes already here by the time the Angles and Saxons (and Jutes/Danes) arrived in AD 4th–6th centuries, but these were the large migrations. Of course, other Germanic settlers have arrived there since the Angles and Saxons. Then Vikings from Scandinavia brought Germanic-laced languages.

3   Even Aramaic has similarities to Hebrew, and this is likely due to the descendants of Abraham and Lot (e.g., Israelites, Ishmaelites, Lot, Moab, Edom, the sons of Abraham and Keturah) conquering most of the Middle East. The assimilation of languages is surely the main reason. There is an "Aram" in the genealogies of Eber, and they would speak a variant form of Hebrew. Though Josephus points out that the Aramean people who spoke Aramaic came through Aram at the Table of Nations in Genesis 10, not the later Aram who was a Hebrew. Aramaic was a common trade language.

4   James Anderson, *Royal Genealogies*, (James Bettenham, 1732), pp. 3, 5, 380.

5   It is possible that the language of Aramaic (the language of the Syrians and that which Jesus cried out in on the cross) is also an Eber language due to its being so similar to Hebrew. Josephus places this language as coming from Aram, the son of Shem in Genesis 1, as a new language. However, due to its similarities with Hebrew and other Eber languages, Aramaic may have been from Aram, the great nephew of Abraham; who was the son of Kemuel, the son of Nahor (Abraham's brother). These people were also Hebrews so it would make sense why this language is so similar.

6   Vistawide, "World Language Families," vistawide.com/languages/language_families_statistics1.htm.

7   Ethnologue, "Statistical Summaries," ethnologue.com/ethno_docs/distribution.asp?by=family.

8   Anderson, *Royal Genealogies*, p. 380.

9   Creationists and evolutionists agree that there was an ice age. The secular side has many of them reaching far into the past, but creationists have one major ice age triggered by the flood of Noah's day. An ice age takes water out of the ocean and deposits it on land, so the ocean level drops, which exposes land bridges, like the Bering Sea Land Bridge.

10 W.T. Fitch, "The Evolution of Language," *NewScientist*, December 4, 2010, pp. ii–viii; available online at newscientist.com/data/doc/article/dn19554/instant_expert_6_-_the_evolution_of_language.pdf.

11 C. Kenneally, "Talking Heads," *NewScientist*, May 29, 2010, pp. 32–35.

12 For facts about Koko, visit koko.org/friends/meet_koko.html.

13 Fitch, "The Evolution of Language," newscientist.com/data/doc/article/dn19554/instant_expert_6_-_the_evolution_of_language.pdf.

14 For facts about Chandrah Leah, visit pethall.com/chanda_leah-tricks.htm and pethall.com/chanda_leah_doorway.htm.

15 Bodie Hodge, *The Fall of Satan*, (Green Forest, AR: Master Books, 2011), pp. 112–115.

16 Charles Duke Yonge, *The Works of Philo: Complete and Unabridged* (Peabody: Hendrickson, 1996), S. 235.

17 Yes, the Chinese originally believed in one God, and ShangDi was likely the name in the Chinese language for the God of the Bible. Information about God and sacrifice from Genesis left Babel and went with the Chinese and remained with them for many centuries. Unlike many cultures that became pagan fairly soon after Babel, the Chinese remained faithful for quite some time. It would be nice to see the gospel, the fulfillment of the promises in Genesis and the Old Testament, reach the Chinese people to bring them back to God.

18 I suggest books by some of the previously mentioned authors, such as Ethel Nelson, Richard Broadberry, and Ginger Tong Chock's *God's Promise to the Chinese* (Read Books Publisher, 1997) or *Oracle Bones Speak* (2012). This second book is jointly English and Chinese and publisher information is given in Chinese, so please forgive the lack of publication information. These authors have been involved in several books on the subject and any would be good for study.

Nimrod's Rebellion

Was Nimrod in charge of forcing a rebellion prior to the events in Genesis 11:1–9?

Introduction

This is a good time to discuss a controversial subject regarding Nimrod. In today's church, many people readily repeat the claim that Nimrod was the instigator at Babel. In fact, if one were to research this, it is not a new idea. About 100 years ago, the Reverend Alexander Hislop presents this idea in his book *The Two Babylons*:

> As the Babel builders, when their speech was confounded, were scattered abroad on the face of the earth, and therefore deserted both the city and the tower which they had commenced to build, Babylon as a city could not properly be said to exist till Nimrod, by establishing his power there, made it the foundation and starting-point of his greatness.[1]

Further back in history, a Jewish military commander and historian named Josephus was writing about the history of the Jews by order of his Roman conquerors:

> (113) Now it was Nimrod who excited them to such an affront and contempt of God. He was the grandson of Ham, the son of Noah—a bold man, and of great strength of hand. He persuaded them not to ascribe to God, as if it was through his means they were happy, but to believe that it was their own courage which procured that happiness.

(114) He also gradually changed the government into tyranny, seeing no other way of turning men from the fear of God, but to bring them into a constant dependence on his power. He also said he would be revenged on God, if he should have a mind to drown the world again; for that he would build a tower too high for the waters to be able to reach! and that he would avenge himself on God for killing their forefathers![2]

In fact, other Jews like the Targum of Jonathan also repeat such things as Nimrod being the one to rebel and challenge God. But let's turn to the Word of God to separate fact from fiction.

What Does God's Word Say?

[1] Now the *whole earth* had one language and the same words. [2] And as people migrated from the east, *they* found a plain in the land of Shinar and settled there. [3] And *they* said to *one another*, "Come, let *us* make bricks, and burn them thoroughly." And *they* had brick for stone, and bitumen for mortar. [4] Then *they* said, "Come, let *us* build *ourselves* a city and a tower with its top in the heavens, and let *us* make a name for *ourselves*, lest *we* be dispersed over the face of the whole earth."

[5] And the LORD came down to see the city and the tower, which the *children of man* had built. [6] And the LORD said, "Behold, they are *one people*, and *they* have all one language, and this is only the beginning of what *they* will do. And nothing that *they* propose to do will now be impossible for *them*. [7] Come, let us go down and there confuse their language, so that they may not understand *one another's* speech." [8] So the LORD dispersed *them* from there over the face of all the earth, and *they* left off building the city. [9] Therefore its name was called Babel, because there the LORD confused the language of *all the earth*. And

from there the LORD dispersed *them* over the face of all the earth. (Genesis 11:1–9)

Take note of the account of the events at Babel in Genesis 11:1–9. Nimrod is not mentioned, and the Bible clearly reveals that the people were rebelling *in unison* (see italics) against God's command to fill the earth as given in Genesis 9:1 and reiterated in Genesis 9:7.

Furthermore, the people knew the command and were intentionally trying to defy it because verse 4 indicates they were resisting the imperative to be dispersed.

The point is that the people collectively resisted God, and the people collectively received this mild judgment of confused languages. Nimrod was not forcing the people to do this. They were acting of together (verse 6) to make a name for themselves (verse 4), which is reminiscent of the rebellion prior to the flood where people had their own interests in mind to be men of renown (Genesis 6:4).

So where did people, such as Josephus, get this idea that Nimrod was in charge of forcing a rebellion? Let's look at Genesis 10:

> [8] Cush fathered Nimrod; he was the first on earth to be a mighty man. [9] He was a mighty hunter before the LORD. Therefore it is said, "Like Nimrod a mighty hunter before the LORD." [10] The beginning of his kingdom was Babel, Erech, Accad, and Calneh, in the land of Shinar. [11] From that land he went into Assyria and built Nineveh, Rehoboth-Ir, Calah, and [12] Resen between Nineveh and Calah; that is the great city. (Genesis 10:8–12)

A repetition of this is found in 1 Chronicles 1:10 where it says

> Cush fathered Nimrod. He was the first on earth to be a mighty man.

Researchers note the first center, or the "beginning," of Nimrod's kingdom was at Babel (verse 10). So people logically conclude that Nimrod *founded* Babel and that he was in charge at Babel because this was his *kingdom* (verse 10). This sounds like a brilliant deduction until one realizes that this now causes some insurmountable theological problems.

Theological Problems

The first problem has already been discussed in the previous section. That is, throughout Genesis 11:1–9, there is no hint of Nimrod's charge, and the Bible repeatedly makes it clear that this rebellion was a collective rebellion against God by all the people involved (descendants of Noah) who were traveling east (obviously of Noah's settlement and vineyard).[3]

How could Nimrod be the one who founded Babel when Genesis 11:3–4 says the people were building it in unison? This is a problem!

Another theological problem is that Nimrod would have been obedient to God by filling the earth and scattering. Recall Genesis 10:10. The first center of Nimrod's kingdom was not only Babel, but four places: Babel, Erech, Accad, and Calneh. So there was not one place that everyone was at, but four! So this would call into question Genesis 11:4 where it says they built *a* city and *a* tower. If the above is true, Genesis 11:4 should read "four cities." And this brings us to another related problem.

Nimrod then went into someone else's land and made cities there, too (Genesis 10:11)! Nimrod went into Assyria, one of Shem's son's land (Asshur), and began building and expanding his kingdom there.

But what is the implication of this? Simply that other people such as Asshur must have also been listening to God's command, had been spreading out, and were not at Babel. If such things are accurate, then God would have been in error when he said that all these people were indeed at Babel and made one city, and that they were being disobedient to him by defying his command to scatter and fill the earth.

But the fact is that God is never wrong, which means Nimrod could not have entered Assyria until after the event of the dispersion, where the earth was divided into various languages and people really did begin to fill the earth.

And this is how these alleged problems are solved. The simplest solutions often make all the facts fall into place.

Solving the Problem

When we look at Genesis 1:1–2:3, we find the chronological account of creation. When we hone in on Genesis 2:4–25, we find that this does not follow chronologically. But instead, the bulk of Genesis 2 is actually a breakdown of what is going on during the sixth day of creation. If one mistakenly reads Genesis 2:4–25 as chronologically following Genesis 1:1–2:3, then all sorts of theological problems arise.

In fact, we find a theological problem in Jewish mythology that is a direct result of misreading Genesis 1–2 as though it were chronological. That is the mythical account of Lilith, the supposed first wife of Adam.

Many Jews in the past read Genesis 1 and saw that when mankind was created, they were both male and female (Genesis 1:27). The word for "man" in Genesis 1 is *Adam*, so they understand that he was indeed the first man. Then they read Genesis 2 and find the creation of Eve. So thinking that Genesis 2:4–25 follows Genesis 1 chronologically, they want to know who this first female was (in Hebrew it is *neqebah* meaning "female"). And so mythology takes over and they invent Lilith, the supposed first wife of Adam in Jewish mythology.

Such Jewish mythologies are unnecessary when one realizes Genesis 2:4–25 is a breakdown of what is happening on day six of the creation week, and hence, the female created in Genesis 1:26–28 is Eve. Genesis 2 simply gives us more details as to the specifics.

Why is all of this important? I suggest that the same thing has happened with Genesis 10–11. Genesis 11:1–9 is the chronological account of the events, and Genesis 10 is a breakdown of the language divisions and genealogies of those rebellious descendants of Noah at Babel. In other words, what is discussed in Genesis 10 is actually the result of Genesis 11:1–9, and Genesis 11:1–9 does not follow chronologically from Genesis 10.

This should be obvious since about 78 language families (minimum) are coming out of Genesis 10, and yet Genesis 11:1 opens with, "Now the whole earth had one language and the same words." But if people mistakenly think Genesis 10 precedes Genesis 11 chronologically, then they will be left with problems that seem to elevate mythologies to fill in the gaps. And Jewish mythologies began to fill the pages with Nimrod founding Babel, which the Bible does not say. Jesus warned about the tradition of the Jews (e.g., Mark 7:13), so we need to test everything against Scripture.

But with an understanding that Genesis 10 follows chronologically, then things fall into place and theological problems subside.

All Is Not Lost

Was Josephus et al, completely wrong? Not at all. With a proper understanding of the timing of the events between Genesis 10 and 11, we can deduce that Josephus was essentially accurate but just had the timing wrong.

Nimrod *did* take over at Babel, it just makes more sense that it had to be after the scattering occurred. Pay close attention to Genesis 10:10. The Bible never says that Nimrod founded or began Babel. It says that it was the *the beginning* of his kingdom (with three other places simultaneously).

After the scattering occurred, Nimrod took over Babel and some other early settlements in that area (Erech, Accad, and Calneh) to be the beginning of his kingdom. From there, he entered into the land of Assyria and began building there as well (Genesis 10:10–12).

He *may* have been angry with God and wanted to rebel as Josephus and others relate (the name *Nimrod* literally means "to rebel"), but not necessarily for what happened prior to Babel, but more likely for what happened at Babel. It is possible that as a hunter, his status was likely high, and with the scattering and language division, much of this status was lost. Consider that Esau's status as a hunter was also highly favored by his father. As many have pointed out, Nimrod's hunting capabilities make him capable of being a "hunter of men" or a military leader as opposed to being a more mild-mannered person like Jacob was (Genesis 25:27).

Many have commented on the meaning of "mighty hunter before the LORD" and pointed out the negative connotations behind it. H.C. Leupold, an Old Testament scholar, says of the meaning:

The course that our interpretation of these two verses takes will be determined very largely by the meaning of the word "Nimrod." For the meaning of the verb form *nimrodh*, without a doubt, is "let us revolt." Now the other words employed are, if left by themselves, either good or evil in their connotation, depending on the connection in which they appear. Gibbor may mean "hero" or "tyrant." "Hunter" (*gibbor tsáyidh*) may be a harmless hunter of the fields, or he may be one who hunts men to enslave them. The phrase, "in the sight of Yahweh," in itself expresses neither approval nor disapproval. But each of these terms acquires a bad sense in the light of the name "Nimrod." The tendency of this Cushite must have been to rise up against, and to attempt to overthrow, all existing order. In fact, he must have used this motto so frequently in exhorting others to rebellion, that finally it was applied to him as a name descriptive of the basic trait of his character. If this be so, then *gibbor* must be rendered "tyrant," or "despot"—a use of the word found also #Ps 52:1, 3; and #Ps 120:4, for which passages K.W. justly claims the meaning *Gewaltmensch*. So this inciter to revolt (Nimrod) came to be the first tyrant upon the earth, oppressing others and using them for the furtherance of his own interests.[4]

If one is familiar with Leupold's positions from other comments, he holds to Nimrod leading a revolt and making the events at Babel occur. Though Leupold is right about Nimrod's name and the meaning of the phrase "mighty hunter before the Lord," why assume this is *prior* to the events at Babel and not post-Babel?

Conclusion

To conclude, Josephus and many others since who have repeated the view that Nimrod was forcing a rebellion prior to the language division may not be the best interpretation, and we should always compare such things to

Scripture (Titus 1:14). Though I suggest we not "throw the baby out with the bath water" as some of their conjectures may be valid.

Though much of what Josephus and others have taught is excellent, we need to compare all things to the Word of God with humility as we too fall short—for even I have taught that Nimrod founded Babel and was the one forcing the rebellion at Babel in the past. When we recognize that Nimrod took over Babel *after* the events of Genesis 11:1–9, things make more sense and theological problems are averted.

---

1 Alexander Hislop, *The Two Babylons or the Papal Worship Proved to be Worship of Nimrod and His Wife*, 3rd ed. (Neptune, NJ: Loizeaux Brothers, 1916), p. 23.

2 *Revised Works of Josephus*, chapter 4, Tower of Babel—Confusion of Tongues. 2242 BC., Lines 113–114.

3 The Hebrew word translated "east" (*qedem*) in Genesis 11:2 can mean "from the east" or "toward the east." Either was Babel. This first settlement was in an east-west direction from Noah's original settlement.

4 H.C. Leupold, *Exposition of Genesis*, commentary notes on Genesis 10:8, (Columbus, OH: The Wartburg Press, 1942), p. 366.

How Did Those Scattering from Babel Travel?

Well, let's rule out air travel right from the start! However, it is possible that advanced technology existed in these cultures, such as hot air balloons.[1] But would such things be used for scattering? Likely not. If anything, such balloons were used for surveying and spotting if they existed at this time.

There are several ways to migrate to different parts of the world—over land is the most obvious, but I would not discount sea migration either. Let's take a look at the feasibility of both.

By Sea

The pages of Scripture make it rather clear that there were "isles," "maritime," or "coastland" peoples who came out of Babel:

> From these the coastland peoples spread in their lands, each with his own language, by their clans, in their nations. (Genesis 10:5)

To go from coast to coast and island to island to settle required the use of boats and potentially much larger ships in due time. This may have become their "specialty." Those of Javan (Greece) and his sons, as well as Tiras (known for early piracy) and some Canaanites like the Phoenicians were among the early tribes who settled many coasts in the Mediterranean Sea.[2]

We need to remember that Noah was a capable shipbuilder, as were his sons. Noah lived for nearly 350 years after the flood until 1998 BC (according to Ussher). Noah and his son Shem, who lived 500 years after the flood, would also have been alive during and after the tower of Babel when the earth was divided by languages.[3]

They could easily have passed along boat-building skills or even helped build some boats themselves. Many ancient boats were quite impressive, so it would not surprise me if many people traveled by ship.[4] Some modern experiments have helped us understand that even simple, smaller boats, such as *Ra II* (made from totora reeds), can cross the Atlantic Ocean.[5]

Boats explain how Hawaiian people arrived at Hawaii as well as other islands that have even older civilizations. Mayan history has a legendary leader, Itzamna (who has since been deemed "godlike"), who brought them from the east via the water.[6] It is difficult to say when the Mayan civilization began and when the earlier Olmec civilization (which we know little about) left off.[7] This leader could have been the one who brought the Olmec people to Middle America by boat. Even the language of the Olmec uses a West African script.[8]

Also, some could have come by boat across the Atlantic

Ra II, an Egyptian reed-style boat built by four Aymara Indians from Lake Titicaca in South America, left Safi, Morocco with crew and supplies and landed in Barbados in 57 days. It was led by Thor Heyerdahl in 1970.

from Europe or Africa and mixed (e.g., think of what the Vikings did), or simply followed the sea coast until they found the Americas from Asia.

By Land

From Babel, we would expect that civilizations closer to the region would be settled first and then those farther away. Initial civilizations such as Babylon, Egypt, and Greece were among the first to rise.[9]

The next general areas people spread to were Europe, Asia, and Africa. Of course, there would be obstacles such as rivers and mountains, but nothing that would completely stop migrations in these three continents.

It makes sense that there would be peoples represented from most, if not all, nations having settlements initially in the Middle East. Some families could have packed up and moved farther away over time. Others may have remained and an offshoot family could expand and move away. Acts 2:5–11 points out that representative people of every nation had become Jews, and that both Jews and proselytes were dwelling in Jerusalem during Pentecost. Some of the peoples listed were from quite a distance, and yet still in the Middle East, Africa, and Asia.

Beyond these three continents would be Australia and North and South America. First, most Native Americans likely came across the Bering Strait from Asia to Alaska. Did they swim? Not at all!

Land Bridges

Most creationists believe there was an ice age that followed the flood. Creationists and evolutionists agree for once. We agree that the ocean sea level would have dropped about 350–400 feet as a result of all this frozen water now sitting aloft on top of the land.[10] Of course, there are differences.

In the secular viewpoint, there were many ice ages extending back hundreds of thousands of years. Whereas, in the creationist reckoning, there was a major ice age that followed the flood and was triggered by the flood.[11]

An ice age is a rare event. If we just cooled the globe, we would get a cool globe; but other factors need to be involved to cause the tremendous amounts of snow and ice and cooler summers so that new ice and snow will not melt entirely. This is what caused a successive growth of compacted ice and snow, and hence, glaciation.

The flood solves this problem. Increased heat of the oceans due to continental movements, possible rapid decay of some radioactive materials, volcanism, and so on means there would be more evaporation, and hence more condensation of snow and ice in winter months.

But what about cooler summers? When Mt. St. Helens, a relatively small volcano, erupted in early 1980 (and also in

Remnants landscape revealing the destruction of the ice age all the way to the coast in Sweden near Kungshamn (photo by Bodie Hodge).

1982), it shot fine dust particles into the upper atmosphere. As a result of these lingering particles, this reflected much sunlight back to space and ultimately cooled the global temperature about one degree! This is a very large change considering we usually see fluctuations of a tenth of a degree over the course of years.

Consider this with regard to mountain building (Psalm 104:8–9)[12] at the end stages of the flood, and soon after as the world adjusted to its new arrangements. There still remains the evidence of immense numbers of inactive volcanoes around the world that were likely from this stabilization period. Many of these volcanoes dwarf the size of Mt. St. Helens. The global temperature could have remained rather cool for some time. And let's not forget other factors such as "higher cloudiness, highly reflective snow, and lower carbon dioxide," which could also contribute to a growing ice age and cause this to extend for hundreds of years.[13]

An atmospheric scientist, Mike Oard, has worked on a model for the ice age (Dr. Larry Vardiman has worked on this subject as well).[14] By their reckonings, the ice age peaked about 500 years after the flood (400 years after

The possible global land surface during the peak of the ice age.

Babel).[15] If their calculations were correct, then the peak of the land surface areas would have been about this time as well. In fact, that would correlate rather well with dispersion of people to various places around the world from the Americas, to Britain, to Japan, potentially even to Australia, and beyond.[16]

For the land beneath the Bering Strait to be exposed, the ocean level would have to be lower. And this mechanism is rather plausible. The ice age that followed the flood would be the perfect mechanism to remove water from the ocean and deposit it on land, thus reducing the ocean level.

This is based on the current depth of the Bering Strait, which Oard believes was a bit shallower in the early stages of the ice age. Regardless, there was a place to cross and perhaps *even settle in*.

Any Evidence of Settlements in Land Bridge Areas?

Actually, there is more than one may realize. Many have pointed to the offshore Japanese temple at Yonaguni Jima. Researchers initially heard of the claim and thought it was a natural formation. But upon investigation, they have changed their tune.

There is much evidence that cannot be interpreted without the hand of man's involvement.[17] There are ten structures off this site and also five structures that have been identified off the coast of Okinawa. One such feature is a step pyramid or ziggurat.[18]

Flipping to the European side, a news report pointed out what fishermen have known for quite some time.[19] It was not uncommon for fishermen, using boats like beam trawlers, to bring up things at the bottom of the North Sea, being that portions of it are rather shallow and the nets

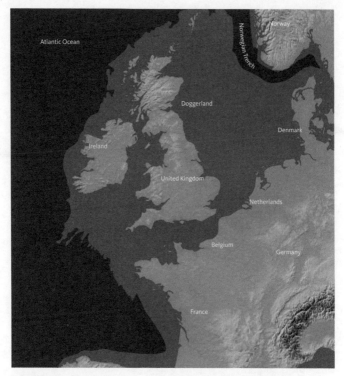

The bottom of the shallow North Sea may have once been exposed
by low sea levels during the ice age, providing a land bridge between
continental Europe and the islands of the United Kingdom and Ireland.
The hypothetical shoreline of Doggerland during the peak of the ice age is
shown on the map above.

drag along the ground. From time to time, they would bring
up artifacts from ancient cultures. Divers have now been
studying the subject and found a number of things, especially ancient tools.

The land was clearly part of the mainland due to lower
ocean levels with evidence of mammoths and civilization
that was ultimately overrun by rising sea levels. One Dutch
archaeologist has accumulated over 100 artifacts already.[20]

Genealogist and historian James Anderson perhaps unwittingly pointed out that residual effects of this were happening up into Roman times near Denmark. He writes in the 1730s of the Danes (Cimbrians):

> But being incroached upon by the inundation of the Sea, They petition'd the Romans for a Settlement in their Dominions, and the Romans neglecting them, the Cimbrians joined the German Nations against Rome, and by their Sword, three Roman consuls were defeated.[21]

The sea had driven them back into Jutland (modern-day Denmark), and even today, the Danes build dams to try to reclaim just small portions of land from the sea.

Many other examples could be cited, but this should suffice to get the point across. This is but the beginning, and an entire book could be published on the subject or even on the undersea findings alone. I would hope more research is done on this subject in due time.

Migration Times

How long would it take for people to travel to the Americas? Oard suggests:

> Sixty years is a crude back-of-the-envelope calculation to estimate the *minimum* time it would take to reach South America. The actual migration would likely have been more complicated and slower. Migration could have happened in spurts. Some tribes could have settled for a while in a location before moving on [emphasis Oard's].[22]

Oard calculates that migrating people could make it to South America in a minimum of about 60 years. I completely agree that this was not the most likely scenario. As Oard points out, the migrations would be slower than this, probably in spurts.

It would take time to travel, as a tribe would probably settle in an area for a while before moving on or, more specifically, before their descendants move along. Many early tribes were probably migrating from time to time too. These spurts would include the time to get to the Bering Strait from the Middle East as well as the time to spread through the Americas. From there, they went south and spread throughout the continent and on down to Central and South America.

So logically, a couple hundred years would be ample time to spread across Asia to the Bering Strait. Many of the first travelers to the Americas probably arrived about 200–500 years after the flood, or 100–400 years after Babel, at about 2142 BC to about 1842 BC (again based on Ussher's dates). It could be sooner for the travelers who went by boat.

In the same way, such land bridges could be exposed to Australia, which has an extensive continental shelf to its north that connects with islands in Southeast Asia and ultimately to the mainland. Of course, it is much deeper in some places that may have been affected by tectonic activity (which is common in that area today). This could have caused it to be much lower today as opposed to the time of the ice age.

There is quite a bit of evidence left behind that confirms the extent of the ice age in North America, Europe, and even other parts of the world. Those arriving by boat—whether from Asia, Europe, Africa, or other places—would not have been limited to the time the Bering Strait or other land bridges were accessible. Some could have come earlier or even *much* later.

1   There is evidence that the ancient Chinese in Asia (unmanned) and the Nasca in Peru (likely manned) nearly 2,000 years ago used balloons. The Nasca people may well have used these to help construct the famous Nasca lines and animal geoglyphs by attaining a height perspective above the desert floor.

2   For more on this, see chapter 16 and the ensuing maps of *Tower of Babel*.

3   We are not certain of the age of Japheth and Ham. The Bible simple does not reveal this information. Many have postulated they lived ages comparable to Shem, that is, unless an accident or disease caused their life to suddenly shorten.

4   L. Pierce, "The Large Ships of Antiquity," Answers in Genesis, AnswersInGenesis.org/articles/cm/v22/n3/ships.

5   *Mysteries of the Ancient Americas: The New World Before Columbus* (Pleasantville, NY: The Reader's Digest Association, 1986), p. 16; and Thor Heyerdahl, "The Voyage of Ra II," *National Geographic*, January 1971, pp. 44–71.

6   Gary R. Varner, *Mysteries of the Native American Myth and Religion*, (Raleigh, NC: OakChylde Books/Lulu Press, 2007), p. 76.

7   There are similarities among Olmec writing and glyphs that are similar to the much larger and later Maya. For more on this, see Mary Pohl, Kevin O. Pope, and Christopher von Nagy, "Olmec Origins of Mesoamerican Writing," *Science* 298, no. 5600 (2002): 1984–1987.

8   Paul A. Barton, "The Olmecs: An African Presence in Early America," The Perspective, theperspective.org/olmecs.html.

9   L. Pierce, "In the Days of Peleg," Answers in Genesis, AnswersInGenesis.org/articles/cm/v22/n1/peleg.

10 Sea Level During Last Ice Age, *Ice Age Now* website, iceagenow.com/Sea_Level_During_Last_Ice_Age.htm.

11 There would have been some minor growths and retreats of the ice naturally throughout this glacial time. One such regrowth is known as the "Little Ice Age."

12 Psalm 104:8–9—The mountains rose, the valleys sank down to the place that you appointed for them. You set a boundary that they may not pass, so that they might not again cover the earth.

13 M. Oard, *An Ice Age Caused by the Genesis Flood* (El Cajon, CA: Institute for Creation Research, 1990), p. 93.

14 Ibid.

15 We would leave open options of this peak being sooner or later. This calculation is good but not seen as absolute.

16 There could also have been tectonic activity that caused some sea floors to become even deeper since the time of the ice age, so it may not be as easy to discern some possible land bridges today.

17 J. Ryall, "Japan's Ancient Underwater 'Pyramid' Mystifies Scholars," National Geographic News, news.nationalgeographic.com/news/2007/09/070919-sunken-city.html.

18 Ibid.

19 R. Waugh, "'Britain's Atlantis' Found at Bottom of North Sea," Daily Mail Online, dailymail.co.uk/sciencetech/article-2167731/Britains-Atlantis-North-sea--huge-undersea-kingdom-swamped-tsunami-5-500-years-ago.html#ixzz234X0Z5XE.

20 L. Spinney, "Archaeology: The Lost World," *Nature* 454 (July 9, 2008): pp. 151–153.

21 J. Anderson, *Royal Genealogies*, published by James Bettenham, 1732, p. 415.

22 M. Oard, *Frozen in Time* (Green Forest, AR: Master Books, 2004), p. 132.

Is "Going Through the Motions" a Saving Faith?

I want to talk about something very important. But let's see if you can spot it first. What is wrong with this short conversation?

> "Hey Andy, have you received the risen Christ as your Lord and Savior?"

> "John, you know I go to church, so of course I'm a Christian."

Did you catch it? Andy didn't really answer the question, did he? And this is a key point: just because someone calls himself a Christian or goes to church doesn't really mean he is saved.

Now don't get me wrong—sometimes a person like this is a genuine believer and simply doesn't realize that he failed to answer the question. It may be good to clarify and ask again even more directly. But other times, people who call themselves "Christians" do so for reasons that are not biblical, such as going to church. They do all the things Christians should, but they do not have faith in Christ. I call this "going through the motions" of Christianity. I had a conversation like the one above years ago, and it made me think about why I call myself a Christian.

I Surprised an Evangelist!

One day during my university years, a Christian from Sweden came up to me and saw that I was wearing a cross. He asked me, "Do you know what that cross means?"

I answered something to the effect of, "It represents the cross that Jesus Christ died on, and Christians often wear them as a reminder of that hope in Christ."

He then asked, "Are you a Christian?"

I said, "Yes."

Then he asked me something that I initially thought seemed a little redundant: "Do you believe in Jesus Christ as your Lord and Savior, and do you believe he was raised from the dead?"

The man's question was insightful because he didn't assume that when someone said they were a "Christian," they had a saving belief in Jesus Christ. I answered, "Yes, I believe Jesus died and rose again to cover my sin and to save me, and I believe in him as my Lord and Savior."

In one sense, I think he was shocked. He was probably not used to getting that answer from most of the people at this very secular university! But I remember thinking that he had great tact in witnessing. Not only was he kind and respectful toward me, which is how people sharing the gospel should act, but he also didn't take for granted that someone who said they were a "Christian" really was. He wanted to find out if I really believed in the Lord Jesus or if I was simply "going through the motions." I have tremendous respect for that evangelist, and I hope that others would follow his example and not be afraid to stand up and witness about Jesus Christ in the same way he did.

Reflecting on What It Really Means to Be a Christian

Over the years, I realized what he meant. Salvation comes by faith in Jesus Christ, not by attending church (though it is important to attend a church), having Christian parents, or living in a "Christian nation." There are many people who *say* they are Christians for these and other reasons, but that doesn't mean they have faith in Christ. They might call themselves Christians because their parents are. I knew someone who was an atheist and has now become a universe worshipping "spiritist" who describes himself as a pagan but also called himself a Christian because his parents were!

Sometimes people call themselves Christians because of their cultural background. For example, in Europe, many atheists still call themselves Christians because of the Christian heritage of Europe. But probably the most common reason is that many people who only go through the motions of Christianity (like sitting through church, going to youth groups, Christian events, and so on) may never have received Jesus Christ as their Lord and may not really believe it in their hearts.

One poll of professing evangelical Christians revealed that 27% of people in an evangelical church do NOT believe in absolute truth.[1] Now consider this: God is the absolute truth. The Bible is the absolute truth. Yet people sitting in pews and going to church are not convinced of absolute truth, and therefore they are not convinced of God and his truth in Scripture!

I hope you are not like this. But if you are, I want to challenge you to rethink what you believe. Here are some great passages you should consider (Romans 10:17 says, "So faith comes from hearing, and hearing through the word of Christ.").

The Genesis–Romans Road to Salvation

Genesis 1:1—God made everything.

In the beginning, God created the heavens and the earth.

Genesis 1:31—God made everything perfectly—no death, no suffering.

And God saw everything that he had made, and behold, it was very good. And there was evening and there was morning, the sixth day.

Genesis 3:17–19—The punishment for sin is death, and because of sin the world is no longer perfect.

And to Adam he said, "Because you have listened to the voice of your wife and have eaten of the tree of which I commanded you, 'You shall not eat of it,' cursed is the ground because of you; in pain you shall eat of it all the days of your life; thorns and thistles it shall bring forth for you; and you shall eat the plants of the field. By the sweat of your face you shall eat bread, till you return to the ground, for out of it you were taken; for you are dust, and to dust you shall return."

Romans 5:12—Because Adam, our mutual grandfather, sinned, we now sin too.

Therefore, just as sin came into the world through one man, and death through sin, and so death spread to all men because all sinned.

Romans 3:23—We need to realize that we are all sinners.

For all have sinned and fall short of the glory of God.

Romans 6:23—The punishment for sin is a just punishment—death, but God came to rescue us and give the free gift of salvation by sending his Son, Jesus.

For the wages of sin is death, but the free gift of God is eternal life in Christ Jesus our Lord.

Romans 10:9—To receive this free gift of salvation, you need to believe in Jesus as your risen Lord and Savior. Salvation is not by works, but by faith—see also John 3:16 and Acts 16:30–31.

Because, if you confess with your mouth that Jesus is Lord and believe in your heart that God raised him from the dead, you will be saved.

Romans 5:1—Being saved, you are now justified and have peace with God.

Therefore, since we have been justified by faith, we have peace with God through our Lord Jesus Christ.

Here are a few other passages worth noting about repentance and salvation (many could be given, but I hope these particular passages speak to you):

For godly grief produces a repentance that leads to salvation without regret, whereas worldly grief produces death. (2 Corinthians 7:10)

The Lord is not slow to fulfill his promise as some count slowness, but is patient toward you, not wishing that any should perish, but that all should reach repentance. (2 Peter 3:9)

Then he brought them out and said, "Sirs, what must I do to be saved?" And they said, "Believe in the Lord Jesus, and you will be saved, you and your household." (Acts 16:30–31)

For by grace you have been saved through faith. And this is not your own doing; it is the gift of God, not a result of works, so that no one may boast. (Ephesians 2:8–9)

Encouragement

Our hope is that you truly give your life to Christ. We want to see people saved from this sin-cursed, death-ridden, broken world. It would be a shame to go through the motions all your life, but never really receive God's free gift of salvation.

The Bible says

> For what does it profit a man to gain the whole world and forfeit his soul? (Mark 8:36)

"Going through the motions" is not faith; it is works, so it cannot save you. You need Jesus Christ, the Son of God, who paid on the cross the infinite punishment that you (and all the rest of us) deserve. Only God the Son, who is infinite, could take the infinite punishment from the infinite God the Father to make salvation possible. We, as mankind in Adam, messed up God's perfect world, and Christ, in his love, stepped in to save us (Romans 5:8). He is a truly loving God.

> But to all who did receive him, who believed in his name, he gave the right to become children of God. (John 1:12)

---

1   Carl Kerby, "WDJS, not just WWJD," Answers in Genesis, May 11, 2000, AnswersInGenesis.org/articles/2000/05/11/wdjs-wwjd. Accessed March 25, 2012.

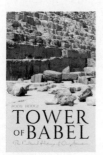

We hope you enjoyed this *Pocket Guide to the Tower of Babel*. Much of this was excerpted from Bodie Hodge's book *Tower of Babel*. If you want to know more, you can find the book at AnswersBookstore.com.

Author Biography

A speaker, writer, and researcher for Answers in Genesis, Bodie Hodge has a master's degree in mechanical engineering from Southern Illinois University at Carbondale. Bodie frequently speaks on topics such as dinosaurs and the Bible, how we can know God's Word is true, and the tower of Babel.

Scan this with your camera app to learn more about the tower of Babel!
GetAnswers.org/babel